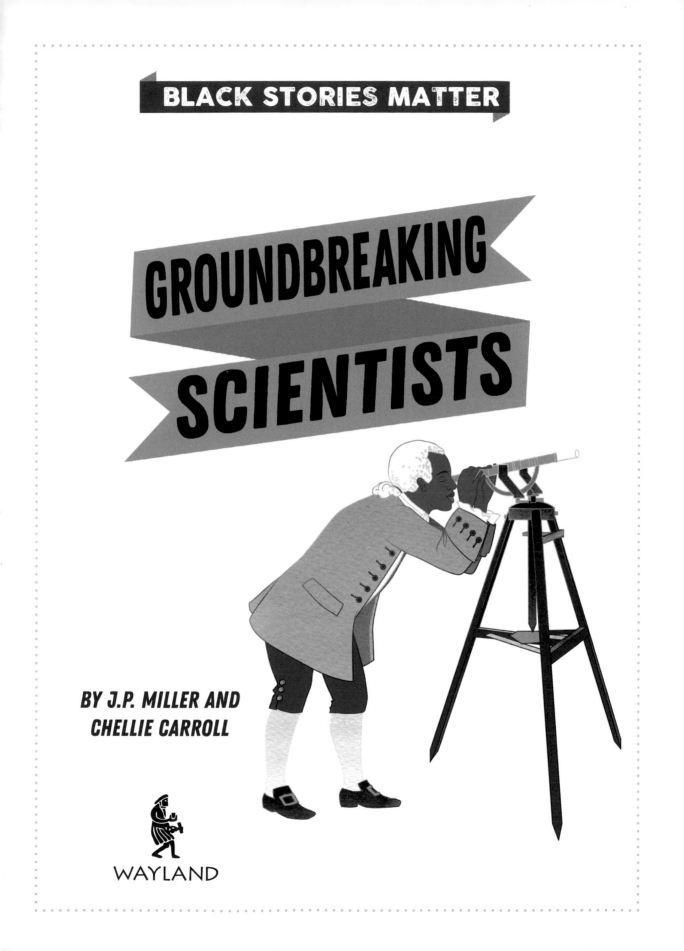

BLACK STORIES MATTER

GROUNDBREAKING

SCIENTISTS

BY J.P. MILLER AND
CHELLIE CARROLL

WAYLAND

For centuries, black people and other people of colour have been labelled as lazy, ignorant or lacking in intelligence. In parts of the USA, from around 1740 onwards, it became illegal for enslaved people to learn to read and write. This was not because they were too unintelligent to learn, as many slave masters claimed. Enslaved people were prohibited from getting further education so they would always have to depend on their masters to survive. But, despite these harsh laws, many slaves invented tools and created new ways to perform tasks that made their gruelling work easier.

In *Black Stories Matter: Groundbreaking Scientists*, you will read the stories of black scientists and inventors from around the world. These brave and ingenious men and women pushed against laws, stigma and stereotypes that claimed they weren't intelligent enough to make a difference. They are only a few of the black men and women who have had an impact on the world with their scientific discoveries. It is their innovative thinking and persistence that allows 21st century people of colour to proudly proclaim … I am clever enough to do whatever I put my mind to!

J.P. Miller is a children's author who is eager to tell stories about little-known and well-known events from the African Diaspora. She hopes that her stories will help to tear down age-old stereotypes and shed light on the many contributions of people of colour throughout the world. J.P. lives in Metro Atlanta, Georgia, USA.

Chellie Carroll is an artist who lives on The Dark Peak in England, and shares her time between her two children, climbing the crags in the Derbyshire hills and producing illustrations that inspire the imagination.

CONTENTS

BENJAMIN BANNEKER

IF MEMORY SERVES ME

The movement was barely noticeable. Benjamin Banneker stared at the pocket watch his friend had lent him.

Tick-tock.

Tick-tock.

Tick-tock.

Time was ticking away. Benjamin held the watch to his ear. He was curious about how it worked.

Benjamin flipped the pocket watch over and popped open its back. Tiny wheels and springs moved about. He committed their workings to memory.

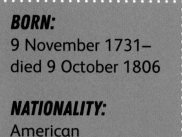

BORN:
9 November 1731–
died 9 October 1806

NATIONALITY:
American

OCCUPATION:
Surveyor, inventor, farmer, writer

Long after Benjamin Banneker returned the pocket watch, the image of its inner workings stayed in his mind.

If memory serves me ....

Benjamin was confident he could build a working clock, and he did.

At the age of 20, Benjamin made a wooden clock that chimed every hour on the hour.

The son of an ex-slave, Benjamin grew up free on his parents' small tobacco farm. Despite little schooling, he showed an early talent for maths, science and astronomy.

Benjamin's talents came to the attention of some wealthy neighbours, the Ellicotts, who moved nearby in 1771. They encouraged his studies, particularly of astronomy, lending him books and equipment.

In 1790, US President George Washington gained permission to build a new capital city along the Potomac River. This would become Washington, DC, the centre of government as well as the location of the White House, the home for each elected president of the USA.

Andrew Ellicott, Benjamin's neighbour and a cousin of George Washington, was hired to help survey and map out the site. Andrew asked Benjamin to help him with this work, and together they measured out the boundaries of the new capital city.

Benjamin also had a good understanding of farming from growing up on his parents' tobacco farm and living in a farming community. So, on his return from Washington, DC., he decided to use his skills to help his fellow farmers.

It wasn't easy for a black person to get a book published in Benjamin's day, but he overcame the odds. In 1791, Benjamin wrote and published the first of several almanacs for farmers. It was filled with long-view weather predictions, farming tips and even some helpful medical advice. He went on to publish an almanac for each of the next six years.

Benjamin went on to become one of the United States' most respected men of African descent.

He saw his new status as an opportunity to address the ongoing injustice of slavery and the treatment of blacks by whites. As proof of his abilities, Benjamin sent a copy of his almanac to the US Secretary of State, Thomas Jefferson, along with a letter in which he said:

"I freely and cheerfully acknowledge, that I am of the African race, and that color which is natural to them of the deepest dye ..."

Benjamin went on to urge Jefferson, who would later become US president, to end the ongoing pain and injustice of slavery in the USA, and to begin to consider blacks as equal to whites in every way. He also respectfully pointed out that the USA had gone to war to gain independence from Britain, but continued to keep black men and women as slaves.

Benjamin died at home in 1806, aged 74. On the day of his funeral, his house burnt down, destroying most of his papers and possessions, including his copies of the almanacs. Despite this, Benjamin is still remembered today as one of the first notable African-African intellectuals and scientists.

DR SEGENET KELEMU

THE DAY OF THE LOCUSTS

BORN:
20 May 1957

NATIONALITY:
Ethiopian

OCCUPATION:
Scientist

The sound of a million tiny wings flapping could be heard long before they were seen. The locusts were on their way to the town of Finote Selam in Ethiopia. There was nothing anyone could do to stop them.

Segenet Kelemu was just a child, but the day of the locust swarm changed her life forever. She watched from the hut where she lived with her family as the swarm of locusts feasted on their crops. Like all the villagers, her parents relied on the crops to feed their family and to sell for money. The swarm destroyed everything.

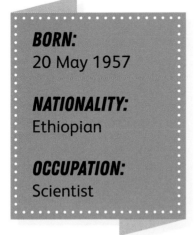

Famine spread throughout the land and crop failures led to starvation and ill-health. Segenet was shocked and saddened by the events. For the first time, she saw herself as something bigger than the small town of Finote Selam.

Segenet decided not to follow tradition or customs. She wanted more for her life than an early, arranged marriage. She wanted to improve agriculture in Africa.

"If you don't have food, then everything else is irrelevant."

In 1974, Segenet packed her things and left home to attend Addis Ababa University in Ethiopia's capital city, where she studied agriculture. She was the first woman in her area to go to university.

Greenhouses filled with plants and insects became Segenet's new home. She became an expert on plant diseases. Her studies and work took her to university in the USA and, later, all over the world.

In 2006, China honoured Segenet with their Friendship Award. It was their highest honour for a foreign expert, awarded for making exceptional contributions to China's economic and social progress.

As Segenet crossed the stage to receive her award, she wanted to shrink smaller and smaller with each step:

"As I was handed a gold medal by the president of China, I felt very embarrassed as they read out all the things I had done. I thought: Here I am from a dirt-poor country in Africa, and I'm making a difference in China."

A voice in Segenet's head told her to think about moving back home, where she could help solve the problems in her own area of the world.

The voice grew louder and more insistent. In 2007, Segenet and her family decided to move to Kenya, where Segenet became head of an international research centre dedicated to investigating which crops to grow where and when, and how to protect crops from insects, such as locusts.

Segenet is part of a new generation of scientists passionate about improving agriculture in Africa and using their work to help fight poverty, hunger and disease.

DR MAGGIE ADERIN-POCOCK

STARGAZER

As far as young Maggie Aderin-Pocock was concerned, the debate was over. There was life in outer space – *the Clangers*! The stars of a British television show, set in space, were all the proof that she needed.

BORN:
9 March 1968

NATIONALITY:
British

OCCUPATION:
Space scientist

Maggie grew up in north London, the daughter of Nigerian parents who divorced when she was four. She moved house 13 times during her childhood, but one thing that stayed the same was the night sky. Born a year before the first man set foot on the Moon in 1969, Maggie was not the only person to dream of being an astronaut at a time of many space missions.

The dream of space exploration inspired Maggie to work hard at school and she even built her own telescope when she was a teenager. But school was actually quite difficult for Maggie.

"My problem with education was that I had dyslexia so I found reading and writing quite difficult."

Some of her teachers doubted that Maggie could ever become a scientist. Scientific study had been mostly done by white men. At times, Maggie even doubted herself. But Maggie's parents' encouragement kept her going.

After she completed her PhD in mechanical engineering, Maggie worked at the Ministry of Defence. Imagine her hanging from the door of an aeroplane thousands of kilometres above Earth, photographing missiles! Although she felt a bit like James Bond, Maggie loved her job helping to construct a missile warning system.

Maggie's next assignment for the ministry was equally dangerous. Many hidden landmines are left behind after wars, and they can hurt people when they explode. Maggie helped develop detectors to find the mines so they could be deactivated and made safe.

Maggie's work hasn't yet taken her into space, although it remains one of her dreams. For now, Maggie's work on huge space instruments, such as the telescopes at the Gemini Observatory in Chile, is the closest she has got to reaching the stars.

> "Every night they opened up the telescope dome just as the Sun was setting and the stars would boldly appear."

Maggie keeps on stargazing. She became the co-presenter of the BBC astronomy programme, *The Sky at Night,* in 2014, bringing her passion for space to a new audience. She also runs an educational company that means she makes regular visits to schools to educate and inspire young people to take an interest in science, especially girls.

GEORGE WASHINGTON CARVER

SERVING THE LAND

BORN: c. 1865 –
died 5 January 1943

NATIONALITY:
American

OCCUPATION:
Agricultural scientist

Life presented some big challenges
to young George Washington Carver.
He was born a slave, he was black
and he became an orphan when
he was very young.

George and his brother were brought up by the slave owners who had
bought his mother. They believed in educating the boys and taught them
how to read and write.

Young George loved to be outdoors. He would go to his favourite spot on
the Carver farm and stay there for hours, exploring nature and working in
his secret garden.

Digging.   Planting.   Talking to his crops.

George was a gifted gardener. Neighbours started to call him 'the plant doctor'. He decided to follow his passion and study agriculture at university.

But George was refused a place by many universities. Then, when he was finally accepted at Highland University in Kansas, as soon as the university learned he was black, they said they had made a mistake and turned him away.

George was determined. He took over some land in Kansas and started planting different plants and crops, carrying out his own experiments and learning through his work. He also studied music and art at university for a year. Eventually he was awarded a spot at Iowa State Agricultural College to study plant science.

After George graduated, Booker T Washington offered him a job at the Tuskegee Institute in Alabama. George was already teaching at Iowa State Agricultural College by this time, the first African American to do so in the college's history.

Once George heard of Booker's offer, he didn't hesitate. He believed it was his destiny to help the farmers of Alabama.

George arrived in Alabama ready to work. He found an old horse-drawn wagon and filled it with farm equipment. He took his mobile classroom out to the farmers.

The first lesson George taught was the importance of growing different crops in a field each year to keep the soil rich and fertile.

"Where the soil is rich, the people flourish, physically and economically."

George showed farmers how to plant and harvest sweet potatoes. Where the soil was worn out with constantly growing cotton plants, George encouraged farmers to plant crops such as black-eyed peas, peanuts and soya beans, to help put goodness back into the soil. These also produced food that could feed farmers' families.

But George didn't stop there. He set up a laboratory to help find other uses for the new crops. Over time, George and his assistants found hundreds of new uses for the humble peanut, including in shampoo and shaving cream!

George's fame as a scientist spread through the USA. He also became known as a campaigner for equality between races. All of this attracted white conservationists and young black geniuses to Tuskegee Institute. George received offers of work from all over the world, but opted to stay at Tuskegee for his whole life.

Thanks to his faith and hard work, George Washington Carver rose from slavery to become one of the most prominent agricultural scientists in the world.

DR MAE JEMISON

SPACE DREAMER

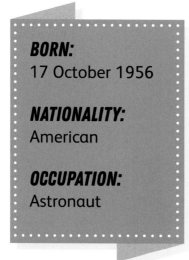

BORN:
17 October 1956

NATIONALITY:
American

OCCUPATION:
Astronaut

Dr Mae Jemison was working as a doctor when she heard that the Johnson Space Center in Houston, Texas, was recruiting people to train as astronauts. Her heart racing, Mae picked up the phone. This was her big chance.

"Johnson Space Center, how may I direct your call?"

"I would like to apply for your astronaut program."

Mae braced herself to hear laughter come from the other end of the phone. Instead, the receptionist simply replied: "Okay, I'll transfer you to the Astronaut Selection Office."

After she had recovered from the shock, Mae quickly gave her address to the person on the other end of the line. Days later, the application arrived.

When Mae was growing up, she dreamed of becoming an astronaut. People tried to talk Mae out of her dream, giving her all sorts of reasons girls could not go into space. She never believed them. Instead, Mae found out everything she could about NASA's Apollo space program and worked very hard at school.

> "I always believed that I would go into space."

Mae had already accomplished some amazing things in her thirty-plus years before she made that telephone call to the Johnson Space Center.

She had studied for a degree in chemical engineering at Stanford University in the USA. She had also studied medicine and become a doctor, volunteered with the Peace Corps in West Africa and become a family doctor in Los Angeles, California in the USA.

But all along, her childhood dream of becoming an astronaut stayed with her.

Out of over two thousand applicants, Mae and 14 other people were chosen for NASA's astronaut training program. She reported to Houston on 4 June 1987, ready for five years of the most rigorous training imaginable.

On 12 September 1992, all the main TV stations in the USA had their cameras focused on Launch Pad 39B at the Kennedy Space Center in Florida. Mae Jemison was one of the seven crew members ready for take-off inside the space shuttle *Endeavour*. She was to become the first African-American woman to fly into space. Her role: to carry out bone cell research and other experiments.

"I didn't even think about being the first African-American woman in space .... I just wanted to go to space."

Eight days and 5,000,000 km later, Mae returned to Earth a happy, but changed person. "The experience made me feel very connected with the universe … My being was just as much a part of the universe as any star or comet."

DRS KENNETH & MAMIE CLARK

HOW DOLLS HELPED END SEGREGATION

One by one, the black children were led into the room. On a table were two dolls with identical features, but one doll's skin colour was brown, and the other's white.

BORN:
Kenneth: 14 July 1914 – died 1 May 2005
Mamie: 18 April 1917 – died 11 August 1983

NATIONALITY: American

OCCUPATION:
Psychologists

Each child was asked the same questions. They were instructed to point at, pick up or describe the doll they believed best answered the question.
"What do you see?"
"A black doll and a white doll."

"Which is the nice doll?"
The child points to the white doll.

"Why is the white doll the nice doll?"
"Because he's white."
"Which doll is the mean doll?"

The child touches the black doll. "Him."

"Why is the black doll the mean doll?"
"Because he's black."

The questions varied.
Which doll is pretty?
Which doll is ugly?
Which doll is good?
Which doll do you want to play with?

The negative feelings towards the black doll remained the same.

Each 'Doll Test' ended with the child being asked to identify the doll that looked most like them. The children all chose the black doll. Most were reluctant to do so. Others became emotional. Some even stormed out of the room in anger.

Dr Kenneth Clark explained the children's behaviour:

> "They were emotionally upset at having to identify with the doll that they had rejected."

As trained psychologists, Kenneth and Mamie developed the test with the aim of showing the lasting damage on black children of educating black and white children in separate schools.

They performed the Doll Test on 160 children between the ages of three and seven during the 1940s.

Kenneth and Mamie Clark met as students at Howard University, Washington, DC, filled with hopes and dreams for a brighter future. They recognised early on that education was key to achieving this. They followed each other to Columbia University and were the first and second African Americans to earn a PhD in psychology in the university's history.

The Doll Test was first invented by Mamie as part of her university degree.

The results showed that children repeatedly thought better of the white doll than the black doll. They concluded that: "prejudice, discrimination and segregation" created a feeling of inferiority among African-American children and damaged their self-esteem.

At the time of the Doll Test the Clarks could have no idea that fifteen years later it would be instrumental in overturning the laws that segregated schools in the US.

In 1951 Oliver Brown took the Kansas Board of Education to court for denying a place at an all-white school to his daughter, Linda. At a later trial, Kenneth Clark's report helped convince the Supreme Court that separate schools were not equal and that segregation was unfairly damaging to black students.

Kenneth and Mamie remained committed to equal educational opportunities for black children. They were co-founders of Harlem Youth Opportunities Unlimited (HARYOU), which focuses on achieving this goal for young people in Harlem, New York.

Kenneth and Mamie Clark also continued their psychological research. They performed many more studies on racial identification among black children. The enormous impact of the Doll Test is still felt today.

The New York Times.
HIGH COURTS END SCHOOL SEGREGATION

BESSIE COLEMAN

THE BLACK AVIATRIX

BORN:
26 January 1892 –
died 30 April 1926

NATIONALITY:
American

OCCUPATION:
Pilot

There was no escaping the fierce Texan sun. Young Bessie Coleman had been out in the cotton field since before dawn. Black people of all ages were hunched over, picking cotton all around her. It was the only way they could put food on their tables.

From a young age, Bessie knew that picking cotton was not for her. But there wasn't much else for black girls to do. Bessie briefly attended Langston University in Oklahoma. She loved it, but couldn't afford the fees.

Bessie decided to take a gamble, pack her things and move to Chicago to live with her older brother.

Chicago was a bustling, busy city. It was jam-packed with black people who had moved there from the south in search of better treatment and a better life.

Bessie studied at a beauty school and became a manicurist at a barber shop. From the moment the barber shop opened until it closed, there was a steady flow of customers.

Bessie listened as the men, including some army veterans, chatted about the great war that was raging in Europe – the First World War (1914–1918).

The black men spoke of all the different types of people who were serving in the armed forces on the same side as the USA, and of feeling accepted as equals when they were sent to France.

Bessie was especially excited to hear about the daring pilots and their fights high in the sky. She decided to find out where she could learn to become a pilot.

No flying school in the USA would accept Bessie because of her black skin and because she was a woman, so she decided to take another risk. She left her old life behind and moved to France to learn to fly.

For over a year, Bessie took flying lessons in France. She loved every moment. When she was in the air, Bessie discovered that she could leave all of her worries on the ground.

On 15 June 1921 Bessie earned her international pilot's licence from the Fédération Aéronautique Internationale, the world's governing body for air sports. She was the first African-American woman to do so.

"No one had ever heard of a black woman pilot in 1919. I refused to take no for an answer."

Bessie roared into the 1920s, performing daredevil stunts at air shows all over the USA. People of all races joined the crowds to see the 'Black Aviatrix', as Bessie became known, perform figures of eight, barrel rolls and daring dives. Bessie made it clear to promoters there must be no segregation at her events. She toured the country, giving flight lessons and encouraging African Americans to take to the skies.

Bessie died in a plane crash tragically young at the age of 34, but she left a huge legacy not just for aviators, but for all women of colour.

"You've never lived till you've flown! The air is the only place free of prejudices."

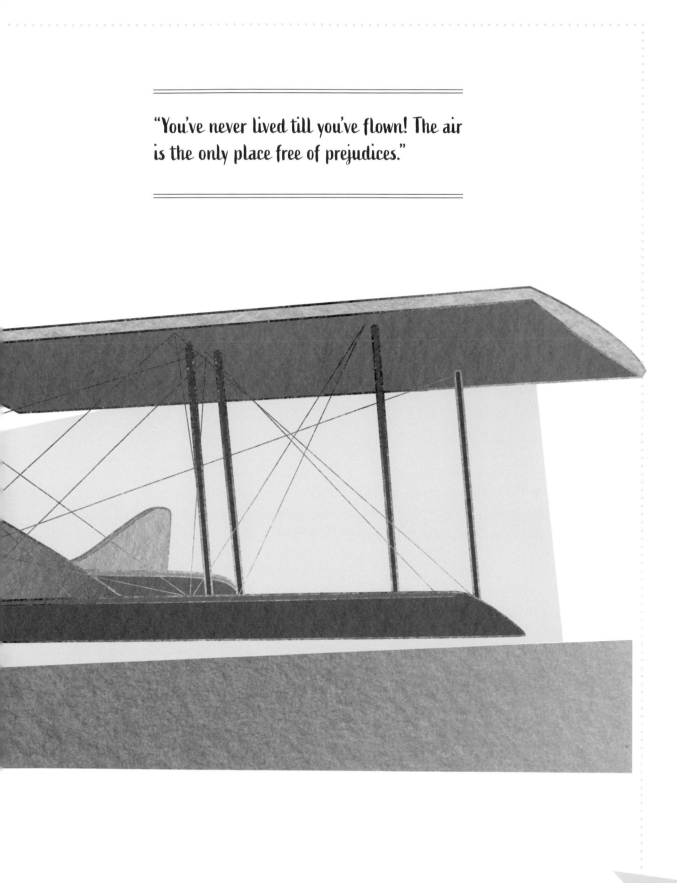

DR DANIEL HALE WILLIAMS

A WORK OF HEART

The year was 1893. The hospital doors burst open and slammed against the walls. The staff of Provident Hospital, Chicago, USA jumped into action. Chief Surgeon, Dr Daniel Hale Williams, examined the patient.

BORN:
18 January 1856 –
died 4 August 1931

NATIONALITY:
American

OCCUPATION:
Surgeon

He did not like what he saw. The patient was an unresponsive black man in his twenties. He had been stabbed in the chest during a fight. Daniel observed that there was almost no bleeding. That meant that the injury went much deeper.

Daniel examined the patient's heart. He discovered that a major blood vessel had been cut. It would take some work, but he believed that he could repair it.

Most doctors and surgeons were against open-heart surgery at that time. It was just too risky. Daniel had to make a quick decision in order to save the man's life.

Daniel made a small cut in the patient's chest with a scalpel. First he repaired a cut to an artery. Then he carefully sewed up the patient's pericardium, the sac that surrounds the heart. He and his team now faced an anxious wait to see if the patient would recover.

Fifty-one days later, the patient, James Cornish, walked out of Provident Hospital. He would live for another 20 years. Dr Daniel Hale Williams had made his mark on history as the first surgeon to perform open-heart surgery.

After hearing of Daniel's work, the US president, Grover Cleveland, made him Chief Surgeon at Freedmen's Hospital (now Howard University Hospital) in Washington, DC in 1894. He wanted Daniel to bring in the same changes at Freedmen's Hospital that Daniel had already made at Provident Hospital. Daniel accepted the challenge and set straight to work.

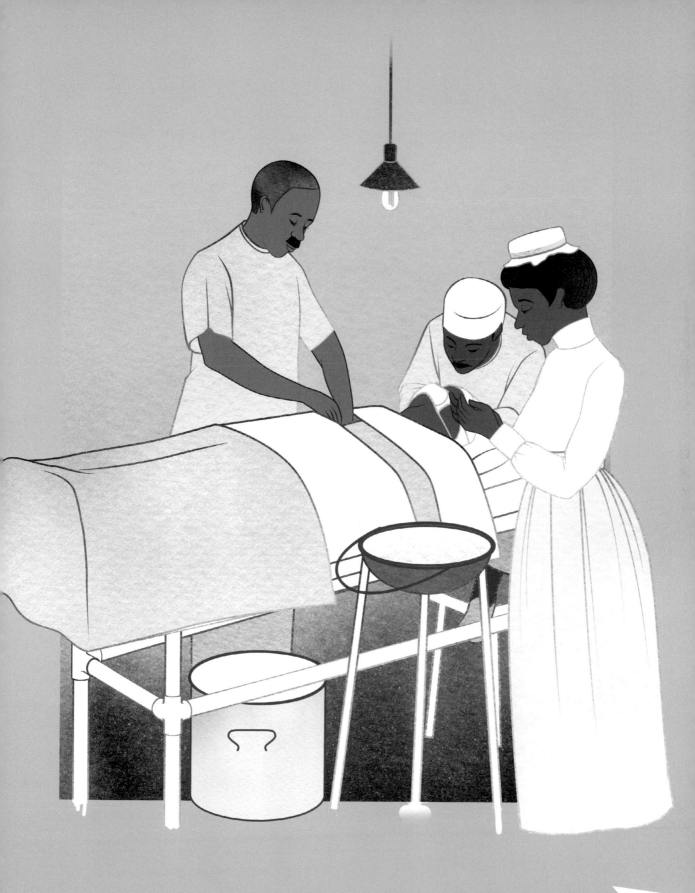

Patient care came first and foremost. Daniel trained the staff in how to sterilise surgical instruments. As had happened at Provident Hospital, patient infections quickly dropped. He established training schools for black doctors and nurses at the hospital.

The Freedmen's Hospital was improving fast under Daniel's direction, but this did not convince the white citizens of Washington, DC to use the hospital. They were not convinced that a black surgeon was capable of caring for them.

Four years later, in 1898, Daniel returned to Provident Hospital and worked in other hospitals over his long career. He performed hundreds of open-heart operations over this time, only eight of which were unsuccessful. In 1913, in recognition of his achievements, he became the first black man to be accepted into the American College of Surgeons.

"A people who don't make provision for their own sick and suffering are not worthy of civilisation."

PHILIP EMEAGWALI

THE CONNECTION THAT CHANGED THE WORLD

Philip Emeagwali was just a teenager, but his homeland of Biafra needed him. Nigeria declared war on Biafra in 1967 after Biafra tried to break away and become independent. So Philip became a child soldier, doing his bit for the Biafran forces.

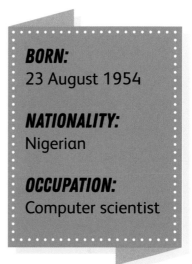

BORN:
23 August 1954

NATIONALITY:
Nigerian

OCCUPATION:
Computer scientist

For three years there was destruction and famine all around him. Philip managed to survive both.

Before the war, Philip had been an excellent student. After the war, he went back to school but his family couldn't afford to keep him there. Instead, Philip's father taught him everything he could about maths and Philip spent his time in the local library, studying. One of Philip's favourite pastimes was to solve a hundred maths problems in an hour!

Philip was soon solving advanced maths problems, so his friends nicknamed him 'Calculus'. Philip's incredible maths skills won him a scholarship to Oregon State University in the USA.

As a child, Philip had been fascinated by honeybees. He noticed that in a colony there were worker bees, drones and a queen bee. Each had a specific job to do. Philip was most interested in the workmanship of the beehive. The worker bees made the honeycomb into multiple six-sided tubes of wax – hexagons. From the bees Philip learned that the hexagon was the most efficient shape for the honeycomb. It used the least amount of wax to build and it could hold more honey.

Philip made a connection between the bees' work and computer science. He believed that if computers could imitate the honeycomb by using the least amount of electronic circuitry to carry out instructions, the computer would be more efficient and powerful.

"It is smarter to borrow from nature than to reinvent the wheel."

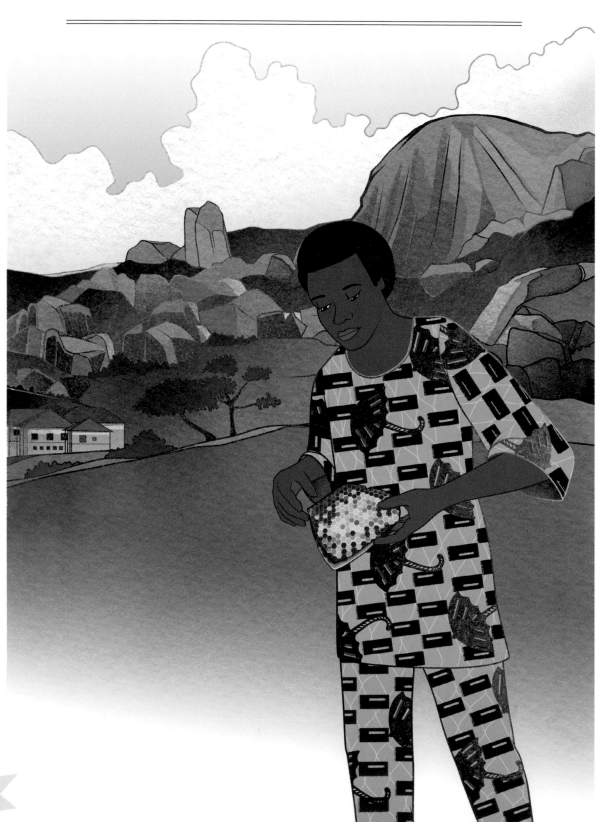

To help with his research, Philip was allowed to use an old super-computer called the Connection Machine at the Los Alamos Laboratory in New Mexico, USA. From his base at the University of Michigan, he accessed the computer remotely, creating different formulas to try to improve the way computers work.

Through his work, Philip created a formula that allowed 65,000 microcomputers to perform 3.1 billion calculations per second.

This breakthrough allowed computers to talk to one another in record time. Philip had created the world's fastest computer. His discovery was essential in the development of the internet.

For his groundbreaking work, Philip has been called the 'the Bill Gates of Africa', after the famous American computer scientist and founder of Microsoft. Philip was awarded the Gordon Bell Prize for computing in 1989.

MARY SEACOLE

MISSION OF COMPASSION

BORN:
23 November 1805
– died 14 May 1881

NATIONALITY:
Jamaican-British

OCCUPATION:
Nurse and
businesswoman

Mary Seacole had already nursed British soldiers back to health in Jamaica, where she was born. When she read in the newspaper that many more British soldiers were dying from disease than from battle wounds during the Crimean War (1853–1856), she knew she had to help.

As a child, Mary had learnt half her medical skills from her mother, a Jamaican 'doctress' who taught Mary how to nurse and treat patients using traditional herbal medicines. The other half she learnt from observing doctors and nurses at work during her many travels.

In the autumn of 1854, Mary travelled from Jamaica to London to offer her services as an experienced nurse. She was turned down by everyone: the War Office, the British army and by an assistant of Florence Nightingale, who was interviewing women who wanted to become part of Florence's nursing team. Many women were turned down because they lacked nursing skills or hospital experience, but Mary clearly had both. This set her to thinking that maybe her nursing skills were being rejected because of the colour of her skin ...

"... Whatever disease was most prevalent in Kingston [Jamaica], be sure my poor doll soon contracted it..."

37

> "Did these ladies shrink from accepting my aid because my blood flowed beneath a somewhat duskier skin than theirs?"

In October 1854, Florence Nightingale and her team of 38 nurses set off for the Crimea (modern-day Ukraine) but Mary was not amongst them. So she needed to find another way of reaching the Crimea. She decided to fund her own trip to the battlefields and she set off on her mission of compassion.

A plan took shape in Mary's mind. She planned to go to Balaklava in the Crimea and set up a hotel for ill British soldiers, funded by herself and a business partner. They would sell hot meals, drinks, food and useful goods to army officers and use the profits to pay for food and medicines for wounded men.

When Mary arrived in Balaklava, her supplies were limited. She had no building materials. So she gathered anything that looked like it could be useful from a neighbouring village and she opened The British Hotel. It soon became popular with soldiers.

As well as running her business, Mary used her own money to buy medicines and food to give to wounded soldiers waiting to cross the sea to Scutari Hospital, where Florence Nightingale and her nurses awaited them. She also rode a horse to visit sick soldiers in army camps and even nursed soldiers on the battlefields.

After the war ended in 1856, Mary returned to London in poor health and with little money. Her unselfish deeds in Crimea were remembered by the many soldiers she had helped, who set up a fund and raised money to help support Mary.

In 1857, Mary published her autobiography *Wonderful Adventures of Mrs Seacole in Many Lands.*

"... And the grateful words and smile which rewarded me for binding up a wound or giving a cooling drink was a pleasure worth risking life for at any time."

Read on to find out more about some other amazing black scientists, both past and present.

DR ALAN GOFFE

Alan Powell Goffe. Now there's an unsung hero! At a time when the deadly disease, polio, was affecting people around the world, Alan played a vital role in the development stages of a vaccine against it.

More importantly, Alan's work as a microbiologist in the 1950s and 1960s helped to make the polio vaccine safe to use for millions of people around the world. As a result, there was a huge decline in polio cases. Alan also helped to develop a breakthrough measles vaccine.

BORN:
9 July 1920 –
died 13 August 1966

NATIONALITY:
British-Jamaican

OCCUPATION:
Microbiologist/
virologist

DR MARIE MAYNARD DALY

BORN:
16 April 1921 – died 28 October 2003

NATIONALITY:
American

OCCUPATION:
Biochemist

Marie Maynard Daly always knew what she wanted to be when she grew up: a chemist! It was a big dream for a little black girl in the early 20th century. Her father's story was her inspiration. Although his own dream of being a chemist was cut short because he couldn't afford the university fees, Ivan Daly set the stage for his daughter to succeed.

Marie became the first African-American woman to receive a PhD in chemistry in the USA. She is celebrated for her research on heart disease and the relationship between high cholesterol and clogged arteries. Marie's work brought attention to how diet can affect the heart and circulatory system and is still relevant today.

DR ERNEST EVERETT JUST

Ernest Everett Just was not a typical teenager. By age 15, he had finished school and college and was qualified to teach in schools. But he didn't stop there. He studied for degrees in Classics, and then English, before being appointed as a professor at Howard University, Washington, D.C., USA.

Three years later Ernest was asked to run the biology department at Howard and his interest in science flourished. He decided to study for a PhD in biology alongside his new job as a researcher at Woods Hole Research Center in Massachusetts.

BORN:
14 August 1883 – died 27 October 1941

NATIONALITY:
American

OCCUPATION:
Zoologist

Ernest is best known for his research on marine invertebrates, which showed that an egg's surface plays an important role in its fertilisation and development. Although the colour of his skin kept him from working at leading universities in the USA, his fame took him to work at research institutes in Italy and Germany. He was the first African American to receive world-wide fame for his work and the winner of the National Association for the Advancement of Colored People's 1915 Springarn Medal for his contributions to science.

JESSE RUSSELL, SR

Forty years ago, virtually no one owned a mobile phone. Today, around five billion of the world's eight billion people have mobile phones. Jesse Russell played a big part in putting mobile phones into the hands of the people.

Although Martin Cooper invented the first mobile phone in 1973, Jesse came up with the idea of wireless phones, as, until that time, mobile phones only worked through technology in people's cars. Jesse has made numerous innovations to improve wireless communications since the late 1980s and received many awards for his scientific and engineering inventions.

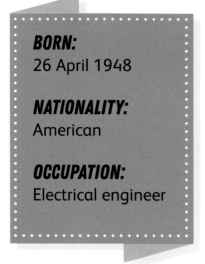

BORN:
26 April 1948

NATIONALITY:
American

OCCUPATION:
Electrical engineer

DAVID UNAIPON

BORN:
28 September 1872 –
died 7 February 1967

NATIONALITY:
Australian

OCCUPATION:
Inventor, writer

David Unaipon was a talented Aboriginal Australian inventor, preacher, writer and scientist. He was known as 'Australia's Leonardo', after the famous artist and inventor, Leonardo da Vinci.

An improved hand-held tool for shearing sheep is David's most recognised invention. He patented the shears in 1909 and went on to patent nine other inventions, although he did not have the money to complete the patenting process.

David's book, *Legendary Tales of the Australian Aborigines*, was published after his death, making him the first Aboriginal Australian to have their book in print. His main mission in life was to spread the message of Christianity and he also worked with people in government for better treatment of Aboriginal Australians. David's face is printed on one side of the AU$50 bank note, along with some symbols of Aboriginal culture and his book.

DR WANGARI MAATHAI

BORN:
1 April 1940 – died
25 September 2011

NATIONALITY:
Kenyan

OCCUPATION:
Environmentalist

Dr Wangari Maathai was proof that just one person can make a big difference. As the first woman from East and Central Africa to be awarded a PhD, Wangari used her knowledge to help Kenyans.

After her studies, she became a professor at the University of Nairobi. She became increasingly interested in finding ways to help the rural women of Kenya, who were struggling to find fuel, water or grow crops to feed their families. Wangari realised that the main problem was deforestation.

Wangari asked the women to join together to plant trees. This was the beginning of the Green Belt Movement, an organisation dedicated to environmental conservation, reducing poverty and defending human rights. Wangari moved into Kenyan politics, where she held several important positions in government. In 2004, Wangari became the first African woman to be awarded the Nobel Peace Prize.

"We cannot tire or give up. We owe it to the present and future generations of all species to rise up and walk!"

DR GLADYS WEST

Dr Gladys West grew up in a small farming town in Virginia, USA, where, after leaving school, most people worked on tobacco farms or in tobacco factories. Not Gladys. She wanted to do something different with her brain. So she worked hard at school and won a scholarship to allow her to study maths at university.

Gladys went on to work for the Naval Surface Warfare Center in Virginia, USA. She collected data from satellites, work that eventually led to the development of GPS (Global Positioning System). Without Gladys' and other people's contributions we would all be lost! From finding ways out of traffic jams to using a jogging app on our mobile phones, GPS is with us everywhere we go.

BORN:
c.1930

NATIONALITY:
American

OCCUPATION:
Mathematician

"You're always competing and trying to survive because you're in a different group of people."

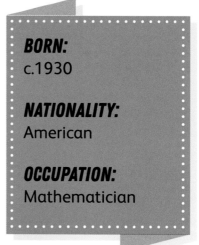

DR RACHEL WATKINS

BORN:
Unknown

NATIONALITY:
American

OCCUPATION:
Anthropologist

As an undergraduate student, Dr Rachel Watkins knew she was about to work on something monumental. She was hired as a bones assistant on the New York African Burial Ground Project. Her job was to excavate and study a mass grave for free and enslaved Africans buried between the 1690s and 1794.

The site had been discovered in 1991 when the City of New York authorities carried out an archaeological survey before starting work on an office block.

Rachel and her colleagues removed the remains from the site and studied them. The bones told the stories of the living conditions and health of Africans in the USA at the beginning of the slave trade. All the remains were photographed and later reburied in a special ceremony.

Today Rachel is a professor of anthropology at the American University, Washington DC, USA.

GLOSSARY

Aboriginal Australian a person descended from the first people of Australia

agriculture the science and work of farming, growing crops and raising livestock (animals)

anthropology the study of humans and cultures (traditions, beliefs and way of life)

artery one of the blood vessels (tubes) that carry blood away from the heart

astronomy the study of the night sky, including the Sun, Moon, stars and planets

Biafra one of the states of Nigeria

blood vessel one of the tubes that carries blood around an animal

Clangers a family of made-up creatures living on a planet in space, the stars of a children's TV series from 1969–1972

Classics the study of ancient Greek and Latin, and the worlds of ancient Rome and Greece

conservationist someone who is active in trying to protect the natural world

Crimean War a war fought by Britain, France and Turkey against the Russian Empire between 1853 and 1856

crop a plant grown in large quantities for food, such as rice, wheat, coffee

custom the language, beliefs, music, art and usual ways of doing things in a place

deforestation cutting down the trees in an area

dyslexia difficulty with reading and spelling that does not affect intelligence

famine when a large group of people have no food to eat over a period of time, leading to starvation

fertilisation when an egg and sperm (or other sex cell) join together to start to make the next generation

First World War the war that broke out in Europe and spread around the world during 1914–1918

Florence Nightingale Florence took a team of nurses out to Scutari (now Constantinople in Turkey) to nurse wounded British soldiers who were fighting in the Crimean War - see above.

formula letters, number or symbols that represent a scientific or mathematical rule or law

herbal medicine pills, medicine or creams made from herbs or plants to prevent or treat illness

independence freedom from the control of another country

integration mixing people together who had previously been kept apart, due to their race, religion etc

Jamaica an island country in the Caribbean Sea, Jamaica was part of the British Empire from 1707–1962

landmine a bomb buried just under the ground, or on the ground, that will explode when someone steps on, or drives over, it

legacy what someone leaves behind when they die

marine invertebrate any animal with no backbone that lives in the sea

microbiologist a scientist who studies micro-organisms such as bacteria and fungi

Nobel Peace Prize an international prize awarded to recognise someone's work towards world peace

observatory building with telescopes and other equipment used to study the night sky

patent this is granted by a government to an inventor, giving the inventor the right to stop others from making, using or selling the invention, without permission

Peace Corps a US government organisation that sends volunteers to help the people of poor countries

PhD short for Doctor of Philosophy, a high-level university degree

polio an infectious disease that can cause someone to temporarily or permanently lose the ability to move part of their body

poverty having little money or belongings - being poor

prejudice hatred for, or unfair treatment of, a person or group of people without cause or reason

psychologist an expert who studies the human mind, emotions and behaviour

research institute an organisation dedicated to research and education

rural connected to the countryside

scalpel a small sharp knife used by doctors and vets to perform operations

scholarship an amount of money given to someone to help pay for their education

segregation in the USA during the 19th and 20th centuries, the system of separating white Americans from black Americans in order to deny them equal opportunities in education, health, housing and other areas of life

shearing cutting the wool of a sheep with shears or another tool

survey to record the features of a landscape or area

swarm a huge group of moving insects

vaccine a special substance that protects a person against a disease

FURTHER INFORMATION

Books
Black History Matters by Robin Walker (Franklin Watts, 2019)
Black Women in Science by Kimberley Brown Pellum (Rockridge Press, 2019)
Young, Gifted and Black by Jamia Wilson and Andrea Pippins (Wide-Eyed Editions, 2018)

Websites and videos
Find out more about **Mary Seacole** at: www.maryseacoletrust.org.uk
Discover some of **George Washington Carver's** amazing peanut inventions at:

tuskegee.edu/support-tu/george-washington-carver/carver-peanut-products
Learn more about **Mae Jemison's** space story at: www.youtube.com/watch?v=tCMJW-auEhE

The website addresses (URLs) included in this book were valid at the time of going to press. However, it is possible that contents or addresses may have changed since the publication of this book. No responsibility for any such changes can be accepted by either the author or the Publisher.

QUOTE SOURCES

Benjamin Banneker: p.8: 'I freely and cheerfully…' https://blackthen.com/benjamin-bannekers-1791-letter-thomas-jefferson-jeffersons-reply/. **Segenet Kelumu**: p.10: 'If you don't have food…' Gates, Bill. "No Mask or Caps, But these Heroes Are Saving the World" Gates Notes Blog. January 4, 2018. Digital/Video; p.10: 'As I was handed…' VPRO Documentary. "Dreams that Inspired Great Discoveries" Video, Youtube. **Dr Maggie Aderin-Pocock**: p.13: 'My problem with education…' Armstrong, Simon, "New Sky at Night Presenter," BBC, December 13, 2013. Digital; p.14: 'Every night they opened…' The Royal Institute, 'Ri Unconference: Maggie Aderin-Pocock - Science and Careers,' December 8, 2011. Digital. **George Washington Carver**: p.17: 'Where the soil…' Iowa Public Television, "George Washington Carver: An Uncommon Life," May 8, 2028. Digital. **Dr Mae Jemison**: p.19: 'I always believed…' Keoghan, Phil, "BUCKit #15: Mae Jemison: First Female African American Astronaut," September 26, 2018. Digital; p.21: 'I didn't even think about…' Nova's Secret Life of Scientist and Engineers, " Mae Jemison: I Wanted to Go Into Space," July 31, 2014. Digital. **Drs Mamie & Kenneth Clark**: p.23: 'They were emotionally upset…' CSPAN, "Landmark Cases: Brown vs Board Doll Test,"

November 23, 2015. Digital. **Bessie Coleman:** p.27: 'No one had ever heard…' Bradner, Liesl, "Meet the Daring Women of Color Who Beat Bigotry in Aviation," July 24, 2019. Digital; p.29: 'You've never lived…' Evans, Ilene, "Bessie Coleman- Portrayed by Ilene Evans," Digital. **Dr Daniel Hale Williams:** p.32: 'A people who don't…' www.columbiasurgery.org. **Philip Emeagwali**: p.34: "It is smarter…' Bellis, Mary, "The Life of Philip Emeagwali-Supercomputers," The Inventors.org, Digital. **Mary Seacole:** p.37: 'Whatever disease…' Seacole, Mary and Sara Salih, 'Wonderful Adventures of Mrs. Seacole In Many Lands,' Penguin Classics, November 29, 2005; p.38: 'Did these ladies…' Seacole, Mary and Sara Salih, 'Wonderful Adventures of Mrs. Seacole In Many Lands,' Penguin Classics, November 29, 2005; '…And the grateful words…' Seacole, Mary and Sara Salih, 'Wonderful Adventures of Mrs. Seacole In Many Lands,' Penguin Classics, November 29, 2005. **Dr Wangari Maathai:** p.43: 'We cannot tire…' www.greenbeltmovement.org. **Dr Gladys West:** p.44: 'You're always competing…' Butterfly, Amelia '100 Women: Gladys West – The Hidden Figure of GPS' BBC News, 20 May 2018.

INDEX

First published in Great Britain
in 2020 by Wayland
Copyright © Hodder and Stoughton, 2020
All rights reserved

Series editor: Julia Bird
Designer: Peter Scoulding
Artist: Chellie Carroll

ISBN: 978 1 5263 1380 5

Wayland
An imprint of Hachette Children's Group
Part of Hodder and Stoughton
Carmelite House
50 Victoria Embankment
London EC4Y 0DZ

An Hachette UK Company
www.hachette.co.uk
www.hachettechildrens.co.uk

Printed in Dubai

MIX
Paper from
responsible sources
FSC® C104740